THE RADIANT YOU

A MINDSET MAKEOVER WORKBOOK

Welcome

Ready for a Mindset Makeover?
Just like updating your wardrobe or giving your living room a fresh look, it's time for a mindset refresh. This is your chance to clear out the clutter, toss away outdated beliefs, and ditch that emotional baggage that's taking up space. It's time to make room for the life you truly desire.

By the time you finish this workbook, you'll be a calmer, happier, more fearless, and more grateful version of yourself—no magic wand required, just your pen.

Think of this workbook as a spa day for your mindset. It's not about changing who you are—it's about enhancing what's already amazing, letting go of the baggage that no longer serves you, and creating space for new growth, new joy, and new possibilities.

Whether you're diving into this workbook for your own personal growth, gifting it to someone embarking on a new chapter, treating yourself to a mindset makeover for your birthday, or starting fresh for the new year—this workbook is designed to help you reflect deeply and reconnect with your awesome self in a whole new way.

So grab your favorite drink—whether it's tea, coffee, or something you'd never admit to drinking in public. Find a cozy spot to relax, find the special pen that is too pretty to use, and get ready to spend some quality time with the most important person in your life: YOU.

This is your opportunity for a mindset makeover—one that'll help you manifest the life you've always dreamed of.

Enjoy the transformation—you totally deserve it!

How The Radiant You Workbook Came to Life

The Radiant You workbook is a natural extension of the wisdom shared in our book, *Conversations with Mom: Recipes for Self-Help*. These powerful nuggets of advice passed from mother to daughter transformed my (Amani's) life, helping me shift my mindset, overcome doubts, and manifest my best life. Inspired by these life-changing lessons, I created this workbook to help others not just reflect, but take actionable steps to transform their mindset and lives.

If you're curious to dive deeper into these heartfelt conversations and the lessons that sparked this workbook, check out *Conversations with Mom: Recipes for Self-Help*.

Amani Aseel
& Sona Seraj

Table
Of Contents

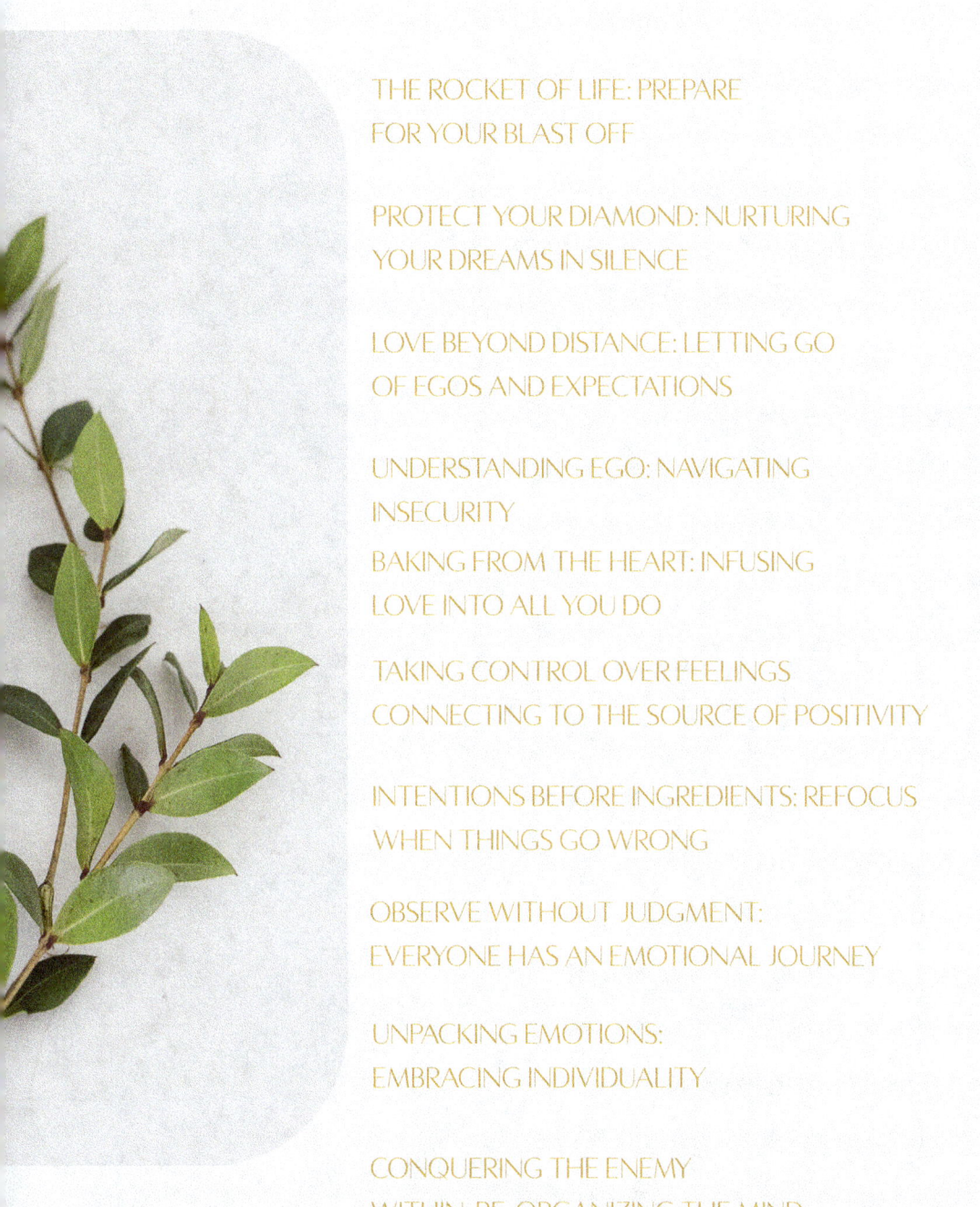

THIS BOOK BELONGS TO THE RADIANT:

_____

The Rocket Of Life: Prepare For Your Blast Off

Your life is like a rocket. You need the sparks, the ignition, and the fire to build until finally, the explosion propels the rocket through the nozzle. Those explosions are similar to the hardships we face while still in one place, serving as catalysts for us to discover our true calling in the universe. Many people endure difficulties and eventually recover, launching themselves toward their destined accomplishments.

OBJECTIVE

This exercise encourages you to Reflect on where you are now and how you can use challenges you are facing to propel yourself forward.

PREPARE FOR YOUR BLAST OFF

01   **What is your True Calling or Ultimate Goal**

02   **Where Are You in the Rocket Process?**

03   **The Challenges: Sparks or Explosions**

04   **Using Challenges to Propel Forward**

Prepare
For Your Blast Off

Take a moment to reflect on your passion, purpose, or the dream that motivates you.

Where Are You in the Rocket Process?

Ignition

Building fire

About to blast off

What challenges or hardships in your life feel like the "sparks" or explosions"?

Prepare
For Your Blast Off

How can you use your current challenges to propel yourself closer to your goal?

Looking back, what are you most grateful for in your journey so far, even during the "burning stage?

What actions can you take today to move closer to your goals and keep your momentum going?

Protect Your Diamond: Nurturing Your Dreams In Silence

"Daro omorakom be al kitman," In Arabic means, "Manage your affairs in silence." This saying holds a profound meaning; suggesting that when you embark on something significant, keep your intentions to yourself until you've accomplished your goal.

OBJECTIVE

This exercise encourages you to reflect on what goals to keep private, allowing you to stay focused, protect your energy, and avoid unnecessary distractions.

WHAT ARE YOUR CURRENT GOALS OR PROJECTS WHERE PRACTICING "KITMAN" (DISCRETION) COULD HELP YOU STAY FOCUSED AND NAVIGATE CHALLENGES MORE EFFECTIVELY?

goals

_____

_____

_____

_____

_____

_____

_____

_____

_____

_____

_____

Benefits of Keeping Intentions Private

How might keeping these intentions private until completion benefit your journey and protect your energy?

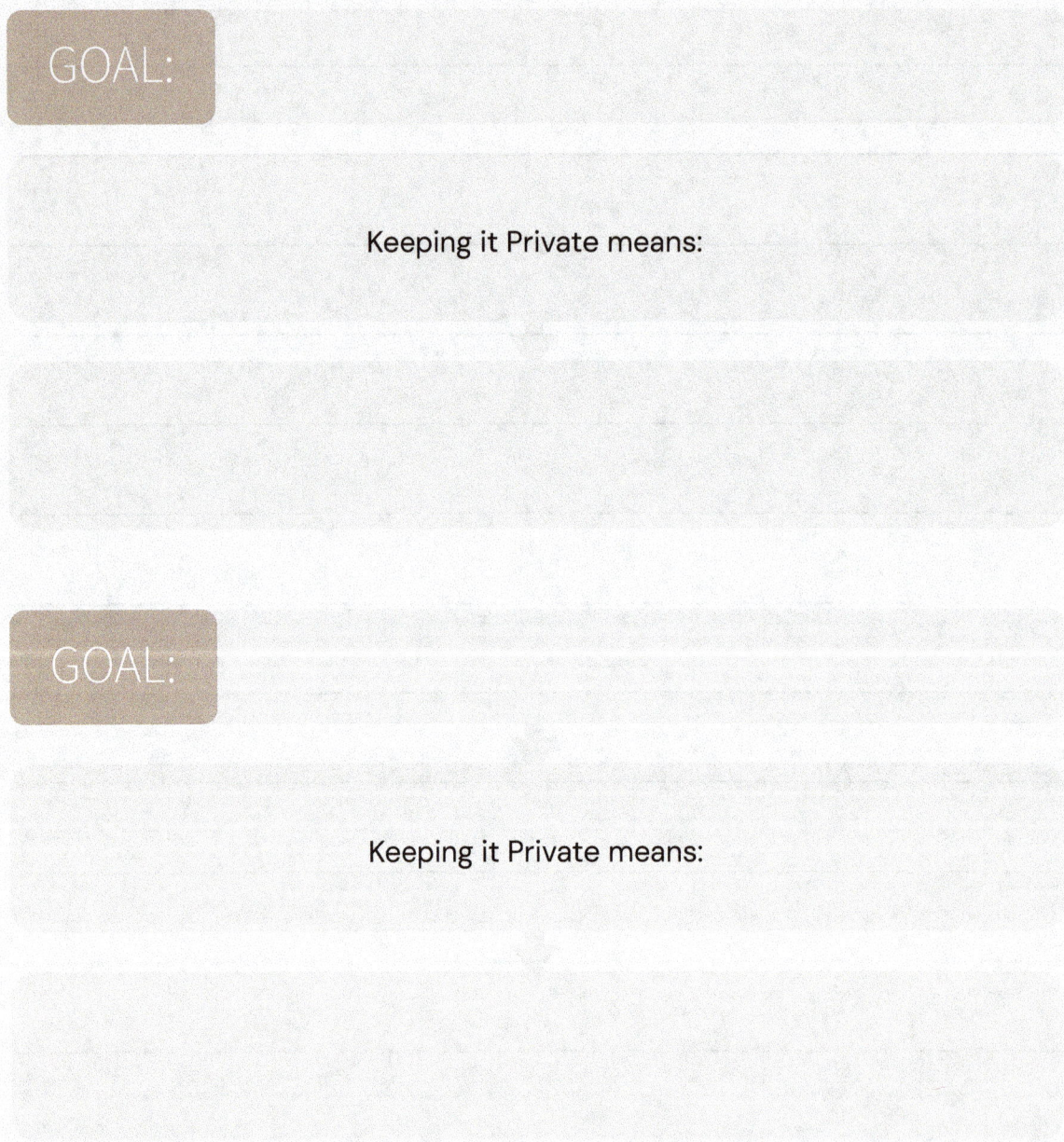

GOAL:

Keeping it Private means:

GOAL:

Keeping it Private means:

Love Beyond Distance: Letting Go Of Egos and Expectations

Self-destruction begins when our feelings don't align with our desires. "True improvements in your life and situation will occur only when your feelings and desires are in harmony."

OBJECTIVE

This exercise helps you notice where your feelings and desires are working together—and where they might be pulling you in different directions. By bringing a little more clarity to that inner mix, you'll be better able to make real, meaningful changes in your life.

The Matching Game

I desire	I feel
I desire abundance in my life.	I feel poor / I feel undeserving / I feel limited.

Take a look? Does it match? If no let's try again match feelings with desires

A Second Chance

I desire

I desire abundance in my life.

I feel

I feel I can do this.

I am open to receiving.

I trust in the process of becoming.

I already carry the seeds of abundance

Understanding Ego: Navigating Insecurity

Ego tends to manifest through possessiveness, especially in relationships like marriage or between parents and children. When we try to control our loved ones' behaviors and view their actions as a reflection of our own success, that's our ego at play.

OBJECTIVE

By taking time to write these reflections, you give yourself a chance to see more clearly how control shows up in your relationships—and how you might gently shift toward more trust, freedom, and mutual understanding.

Control Reflection

Reflect on Control in Your Relationships

Take a moment to reflect on how control might show up in your relationships.

Write down moments when you've tried to influence someone's choices or actions.

What are the emotions behind the need to control?

Reflect and write: What steps can you take to replace control with trust and support?

Baking From The Heart: Infusing Love Into All You Do

Love yourself first and foremost. The more you love yourself, the more love you will have that you can give. And when you give love freely, you'll receive even more in return. It's one of the secrets of the universe.

OBJECTIVE

This exercise helps you be more intentional about staying connected to the things you love. It gently guides you back to a state of love—where you feel present, grounded, and aligned with what truly matters to you.

I STAY IN A STATE OF LOVE WHEN:

HOW OFTEN DO YOU REFILL YOUR LOVE TANK?

How do you stay in a state of love?

ACTIONS CAN YOU TAKE TO STAY IN STATE OF LOVE

Taking Control Over Feelings: Connecting To The Source of Positivity

Don't let your feelings manipulate you, and don't let them take over you. Take control over them to prevent the mess and chaos of your thoughts.

Keep close to your source of positive energy. As long as you stay connected to your source, you will gain control over your life.

OBJECTIVE

This exercise helps you observe, reflect, and let go of a thought or emotion that has been affecting you. By the end, you should feel lighter, calmer, and more in control of your emotional state.

Releasing Thoughts and Emotions

1
IDENTIFY THE
THOUGHT OR EMOTION

Begin by noticing any thoughts or emotions that are on your mind. Perhaps you feel anxious, worried, sad, or fearful. Select one thought or emotion to focus on.

2
EXAMINE
THE THOUGHT

Where is this thought coming from? What is its message? Is it real, or is it just my mind imagining worst-case scenarios?

4
RELEASE
THE THOUGHT

Visualize the thought leaving your body and mind. Breathe deeply, allowing it to drift away like a cloud.

3
ENGAGE WITH
THE THOUGHT

Speak with the thought. Acknowledge it, but also remind it that it no longer needs to control you. It is time to go

5
NOTICE THE SHIFT

As you release the thought, notice how your body feels. Do you feel more at peace or lighter?

6
REFLECT

Take a moment to journal your experience. Reflect on the questions: What emotions arose after you let go? What I can replace these emotions with Replace with more peace, or more joy

Releasing Thoughts and Emotions

1 IDENTIFY THE
THOUGHT
OR EMOTION

2 EXAMINE
THE THOUGHT

4 RELEASE
THE THOUGHT

3 ENGAGE WITH
THE THOUGHT

5 NOTICE
THE SHIFT

6 REFLECT

Intentions Before Ingredients: Refocus When Things Go Wrong

Before diving into any task or adventure, it's important to set our intentions. It's like adding a special flavor to our actions, making them more meaningful and enjoyable.

OBJECTIVE

This exercise helps you create a purposeful mindset before engaging in any task or event, allowing you to approach each action with clarity, meaning, and enjoyment

Setting Intentions for Actions and Plans

Date:

Choose The Task

Think about a task or event you are about to engage in, big or small

Set Your Intention

Ask yourself, what do I want to experience while doing this? How do I want to feel before, during, and after completing this task?

Engage with Your Intention

As you carry out the task, keep your intention in mind. Let it guide your actions, Observe how focusing on your intention affects your experience.

Reflect After completion

Did my intention shape how I approached the task? How did it affect my experience or the outcome? How did I feel while engaging in the task with intention?

Setting Intentions for Actions and Plans

Date:

Choose The Task

Set Your Intention

Engage with Your Intention

Reflect After completion

Setting Intentions for Actions and Plans

Date:

Choose The Task

Set Your Intention

Engage with Your Intention

Reflect After completion

Observe Without Judgment: Everyone Has an Emotional Journey

Attempting to assume someone else's emotional burdens weighs us down. We can never truly know what they are feeling. So, it's important to focus on observing our own emotions rather than fixating on the feelings of others. When it comes to your daughters, avoid over-analyzing or assuming their emotions. Be empathetic without immersing yourself in someone else's feelings.

OBJECTIVE

This exercise helps you practice observing from a distance—offering empathy without getting emotionally swept up in someone else's experience.

Observe Without Judgment

1. Identify the Situation:

Think of a recent situation where you were emotionally affected by someone else's feelings. This could be a family member, friend, or colleague. Write down what happened.

Example Situation:

My daughter came home upset from school, and I immediately felt anxious and overwhelmed, assuming something was wrong."

2. Observe Without Over-Identifying:

Take a moment to reflect on how you typically react in such situations. Ask yourself:

How did I feel when this person was upset?

Did I start to feel their emotions as if they were my own?

How did this impact my mindset and energy?

Example Reflection:

"When my daughter was upset, I immediately felt like I needed to fix things for her. I began to feel anxious and worried, as if I were in her shoes. I lost my sense of calm in the process."

3. Set the Intention for Detachment and Empathy:

Before engaging with the person, set an intention for the interaction. You can be empathetic, but you don't need to absorb their emotional burden. Your goal is to listen, understand, and offer support without losing your emotional balance.

Example Intention:

"I intend to listen deeply and offer empathy, but I will stay grounded in my own emotional space. I will not take on her feelings as my own."

4. Engage with Empathy, Not Drama:

Now, practice interacting with the person in a way that maintains your emotional boundaries. Listen actively without immediately trying to solve the problem or mirror their emotions. Validate their feelings but keep a sense of emotional detachment.

Example Action:

When my daughter is upset, I acknowledge her feelings: "I can see you're upset. It's okay to feel that way." I avoid jumping into problem-solving mode immediately and instead allow her to express herself. I stay calm, and I remind myself, "Her feelings are hers, not mine."

5. Practice Self-Care Afterward:

After engaging in an empathetic interaction, it's important to ground yourself and practice self-care to return to your own energy. This can help you detach and release any lingering emotions you may have picked up.

Example Self-Care:

After the conversation, I take a few deep breaths, go for a short walk, or spend a few minutes meditating to clear my mind and reconnect with my own emotions.

OBSERVE WITHOUT JUDGMENT

Identify
the Situation

**OBSERVE WITHOUT
OVER-IDENTIFYING**

**ENGAGE
WITH EMPATHY**

**DETACHMENT AND
EMPATHY**

**SELF-CARE
AFTERWARD**

OBSERVE WITHOUT JUDGMENT

Identify
the Situation

**OBSERVE WITHOUT
OVER-IDENTIFYING**

**ENGAGE
WITH EMPATHY**

**DETACHMENT AND
EMPATHY**

**SELF–CARE
AFTERWARD**

Unpacking Emotions: Embracing Individuality

Ultimately, the purpose of our existence is to live in joy, love, and happiness. We must do our part and let go of the rest, trusting in a higher power. We can't control every aspect of our lives.

She shared a story about the Virgin Mary, who was asked to shake a palm tree while in labor. The task seemed impossible, but Mary touched the tree and the dates came to her, easing her labor. Mom drew a parallel to our own lives—take action, shake the palm tree, but also let go of control and have faith that things will work out.

OBJECTIVE

This exercise is meant to be an invitation to take small, intentional steps toward your goals, without pressure or perfection. It's a gentle reminder that progress doesn't have to be big or dramatic to be meaningful. Every little step counts.

I can

I can

I can

I can

I can

Imagine you're shaking your own "metaphorical palm tree" what can you do today to take action, but also trust that things will work out in their own time? (No stress!)

Have fun with this! It's all about taking small actions, having a little faith, and letting life surprise you!

Conquering The Enemy Within: Re-organizing The Mind

Deep within us resides a foe that leads us to make poor decisions like choosing chocolate over fruit. We have the power to tame this ever-present enemy of the self just as we control our thoughts, understanding that some drag us into negativity and misfortune, while others bring joy and success.

Curiously, I asked, "How can we overcome this enemy?"

"Awareness is key. We need to pay attention not only to the enemy's presence but also to the ongoing conversation between our self and that enemy. By observing and directing this conversation, we can gain control. It's a gradual process, but with practice, the work becomes easier."

OBJECTIVE

Be mindful of your inner dialogue and shift it toward a more supportive, positive tone that helps you become the person you want to be.

Identify the Current Dialogue:

What are some of the common thoughts or phrases you've been saying to yourself recently?

Is your inner voice mostly positive or negative? How does it affect your mood, energy, and decisions throughout the day?

When you notice negative or unhelpful thoughts, how can you shift them to a more positive or empowering mindset? What's one thing you can tell yourself today to boost your confidence or mood?

The Power Of Gratitude:
Glowing From
The Inside Out

Do you know that a grateful state of mind attracts more blessings, contentment, and abundance? It is the highest mental state, where we feel satisfied and thankful. On the contrary, covering up blessings through complaining or dwelling on negativity tortures the soul. In this state, the mind veils the blessings until they become invisible, leading to suffering, depression, and negative consequences.

If we find ourselves complaining, covering up the blessings, Mom advised that we pause, reconsider, and reset our inner state to one of gratitude. She emphasized the importance of engaging in acts that foster gratitude, such as kindness, prayer, connecting with the source, expressing thanks to others, motivating friends, or helping someone in need.

OBJECTIVE

This exercise encourages you to pause, reflect, and shift your mindset toward gratitude, inviting more joy and positivity into your life.

Glowing From
The Inside Out

Month :

Reflect on your day today:

Can you think of one thing you're grateful for?

Could be something big or small, like a kind word from a friend or a peaceful moment. Write it down!

Pause and Reset:

Have you ever found yourself complaining or focusing on something negative? What's one thing you could do right now to shift your mindset to a more grateful one? (Maybe take a deep breath, smile, or think of something you're thankful for!)

Act of kindness:

What you could do today to spread gratitude. Maybe it's helping a friend, saying "thank you" to someone, or offering a compliment. What's something you can do to help others feel grateful too?

Glowing From
The Inside Out

Month :

Reflect on your day today:

Pause and Reset:

Act of kindness:

Laughter Is The Sweetness Of Life's Cake: Don't Be So Serious

Picture seriousness as an eraser that has the power to eliminate love, fun, and joy. The opposite of seriousness, however, doesn't entail being frivolous, lazy, or inattentive. Instead, it revolves around the concept of avoiding neglectfulness.

Some people are afraid of being seen as neglectful or insubstantial, so they take away the playful side of life and miss all the best parts. It's like making an apple cake and forgetting to add the yogurt, milk, or cream—the result will be hard and difficult to swallow.

We need moisture in the batter of life to make our days light, easy to enjoy, and digest. That moistness consists of kindness, love, flexibility, easiness, and laughter

OBJECTIVE

This exercise helps you become more intentional about laughter, bringing more joy and fun into your day so you can attract positivity into your daily routine.

Adding Laughter
TO YOUR DAY

01

What's one thing you could add to your daily routine that would make you laugh or feel lighter? Maybe it's watching a funny video, telling a silly joke, or spending time with someone who makes you smile. Write down one fun idea!

Picture the "Moisture" in Life:

Think about a time when life felt light and easy, full of fun or laughter. What were you doing, and how did it make your day better? How can you bring that feeling into to today?

02

03

Laughing Without Guilt: Sometimes, we feel like we need to be serious all the time. How can you remind yourself that laughter and joy are important parts of life?

Adding Laughter
TO YOUR DAY

01

02

03

The Head Of and The Tail Of Beliefs: Do A Spring Cleaning Of The Mind

There was a woman who had a peculiar habit while cooking fish. Every time she prepared fish, she always cut off the tail and head. One day, her curious daughter asked, 'Why do you always remove the tail and head of the fish?'

"The mother replied, 'Well, my own mother always cooked fish this way.' Intrigued, the girl asked her grandmother the same question. She explained that she learned the practice from her mother. Consulting other relatives, they eventually discovered that their great-grandmother had only one small pan that couldn't accommodate a whole fish. Hence, she trimmed the head and tail of every fish she cooked to fit in the pan."

Beliefs are shaped by our experiences. Positive experiences create positive ideas, while negative experiences give rise to negative ones. But this isn't the ideal way to form beliefs.

Beliefs can also be shaped by our thoughts. Our thoughts, emotions, and beliefs are like interconnected gears, each influencing the other. It all begins with our thoughts, which then generate feelings, and these feelings, in turn, shape our beliefs.

OBJECTIVE

To reflect on your beliefs—releasing the ones that no longer serve you and making space for new, empowering beliefs that support your growth, confidence, and success.

Spring Cleaning of Beliefs

1. Dust Off the Old Belief

What belief has been cluttering your mind and holding you back?

Example:

I'm not good enough.

2. Where Did This Belief Come From?

Trace its roots. Was it from someone else's words, an early experience, or a cultural message?

Example:

My mother always compared me to others, and I started to believe I wasn't smart enough.

3. Wipe it Down with Truth

Challenge it. Is it actually true?

What evidence proves otherwise?

Example:

I've achieved a lot despite feeling this way. I've overcome many challenges. That means I am good enough.

4. Plant a New Belief

Replace the old belief into something kinder, empowering, and believable.

Example:

- "I am growing and doing my best."
- "I am worthy of love and success."
- "I am enough just as I am."

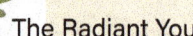

The Radiant You

Spring Cleaning
of Beliefs

Spring Cleaning
of Beliefs

5. Shine Light On It

Take one small action that reflects this new belief.

Example:

Make a "Proof of Enoughness" List. Write down 3 things you've done in the past week that show you are capable, worthy, or growing.

Examples:

- I helped a friend through something tough.
- I finished a task I was nervous about.
- I showed up for myself even when I doubted.

Repeat this process for any other belief you're ready to rewrite. Keep this worksheet handy and revisit it when you need to realign.

Spring Cleaning
of Beliefs

5. Shine Light On It

Take one small action that reflects this new belief.

Action Step:

Repeat this process for any other belief you're ready to rewrite. Keep this worksheet handy and revisit it when you need to realign.

The Flow Of Your Rivers: Avoid Resistance

Imagine yourself walking against the flow of a river. After a while, exhaustion sets in, and you become oblivious to the beauty surrounding you because your sole focus is on battling the current.

Similarly, when we concentrate on negative emotions or our own shortcomings, it engenders pain, dissatisfaction, troubles, and sadness.

OBJECTIVE

This exercise helps you let go of resistance so you can rediscover the beauty and balance within and around you.

IMAGING THE STRUGGLE:

Picture yourself walking against the flow of a river. What do you feel physically and emotionally as you struggle to keep moving? How does it affect your energy and mood?

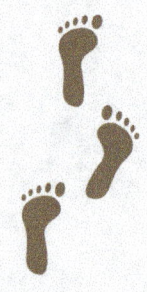

NOTICING THE BEAUTY:

While you're focused on battling the current, what might you miss around you? What are some positive or beautiful things that might pass unnoticed?

FLOW LIKE A RIVER

SHIFTING YOUR FOCUS:

Think of a situation where you've been focused on your short comings. How can you shift your attention to the good things around you instead? What's one positive thing you could focus on today to change your mindset?

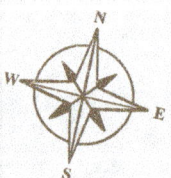

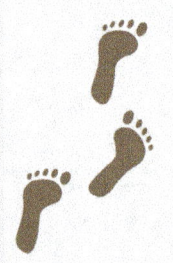

LETTING GO OF THE STRUGGLE:

How can you ease the struggle and stop fighting the current of negative emotions? Write down one action you can take today to accept your emotions without letting them take control, and start embracing a more peaceful or positive mindset.

IMAGINING THE STRUGGLE:

NOTICING THE BEAUTY:

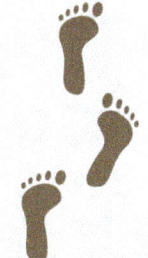

FLOW
LIKE A RIVER

SHIFTING YOUR FOCUS:

LETTING GO OF THE STRUGGLE:

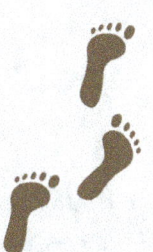

Following Mama Duck: Parents Program Their Children

When we are out of balance, and when negative emotions outweigh the positive ones in our daily lives, we tend to become unhappy for extended periods. We may develop phobias and anxiety that hinder our ability to carry out our daily activities with serenity. In these situations, we are far from the paths of peace, love, and joy. This is the negative programming.

OBJECTIVE

To explore the source of negative beliefs by reflecting on where they may have originated—whether from past experiences, outside influences, or someone else's words—so you can begin to shift what doesn't belong to you and take action toward reclaiming your personal truth.

Identifying The Program

Recognizing Negative Programming:

Think about areas in your life where you feel stuck or unable to make progress.

Are there any beliefs, thoughts, or feelings that repeatedly hold you back. Write down a few examples of negative thoughts or self-talk that may be preventing you from moving forward.

Tracing the Source Of These Beliefs:

Where these negative beliefs or feelings might have come from. Did Someone say something to you that made you believe you weren't capable?

Past experiences ?

Try to trace back the origin of these negative thoughts. Where did they start?

Shifting Your Mindset:

How can you replace this belief with something more empowering or positive?

Shifting Your Mindset:

Choose one small action you can take today to challenge the negative programming and move toward your goal.

Identifying
The Program

Recognizing Negative Programming:

Tracing the Source Of These Beliefs:

Shifting Your Mindset:

Shifting Your Mindset:

Shaping The Life We Desire: Exploring Feelings, Emotions, and Passion

Feelings are small things that come and go, beyond our control. They can be good or bad, and sometimes they don't even have a reason. Emotions can have a lasting impact on us, shaping our lives for better or worse. They can make us feel positive or negative, influencing our outlook on things Passion, however, is a controlled emotion. You are have it intentionally when you start doing something you love. It brings immense joy and positive experiences. When someone is passionate about something, it's evident, and we love seeing it. Passion takes us to a higher level of positive emotions and opens doors to our dreams and desires. It's crucial to find our passion, pursue it, and always be enthusiastic about what we do.

OBJECTIVE

To help you reconnect with your passions by identifying what truly lights you up, understanding the emotions these activities evoke, and taking small, intentional steps to bring more of that joy and fulfillment into your daily life.

Discovering
Your Passion

What activities make you lose track of time?

How do you feel when you're practicing your passion?

What small step can you take today to make sure you practice your passion?

What obstacles or challenges do you face in practicing your passion, and how can you work through them

How can you share your passion with others or use it to inspire people around you?

The Power Of Thoughts: Taking Control Of Your Mind

When you think of a person, you automatically create what I call an 'energy thread' between the two of you. If your beliefs about that person are positive, this thread carries positive energy, and just thinking about them can bring you positivity.

Conversely, if your beliefs about someone are negative, or if they have had a negative impact on your life, you'll experience negative feelings and energy when you think of them.

Conscious individuals can choose whom they think about and how. But what if thoughts of someone you've created a negative connection with keep appearing?

In such cases, you need to be aware that thinking about that person will only bring heartache.

Instead, replace those thoughts with something you genuinely enjoy. It could be your favorite food, a beautiful memory, a satisfying accomplishment like organizing your closet, or even the anticipation of a delicious dinner. Repeatedly replacing thoughts of negative individuals with positive ones will develop a habit of diverting your mind and cutting the energy thread before it becomes stronger.

OBJECTIVE

This exercise helps you recognize how certain relationships impact your emotional state, and offers intentional steps to reclaim your energy, uplift your mood, and create space for more joy and peace in your daily life.

The energy Thread

Reflect on your relationships

Think of a person in your life (past or present) who triggers a strong emotional reaction when you think of them. Do you feel positive or negative energy when their name or face comes to mind?

Describe the energy

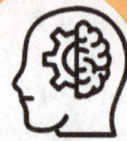

What kind of 'energy thread' have you created with this person? Is it positive, negative, or neutral? How does this thread affect your emotional state when you think of them?

Explore the impact

How does thinking about this person impact your day-to-day mood or actions? Do they have a lasting influence on your thoughts and feelings?

Replace the thread

Think of a positive memory, accomplishment, or something you genuinely enjoy. Imagine that energy thread connecting you to that positive source instead. How does this change your emotional state?

Create a strategy

Write down three things you can do to actively shift your focus away from negative connections and into something that brings you joy.

Track your progress:

Notice when the negative energy thread appears again. What do you do to replace it with something positive? How does it feel after a few days of practice?

The energy Thread

Reflect on your relationships

Describe the energy

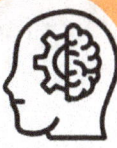

Explore the impact

Replace the thread

Create a strategy

Track your progress:

Liberate And Love Yourself: You Are Complete

Always remember that you are complete just the way you are. Within you lies the power to create your own happiness. You possess every capability needed to find fulfillment. It's essential to understand that no person, family, or material possession can truly complete you. While they can enhance your life, they are not the missing piece. This truth has been reiterated through countless stories of individuals tirelessly seeking external sources of happiness, only to discover that what they desired was within them all along. Remember this, and let it resonate within your being.

OBJECTIVE

This exercise helps you reflect on your strengths, capabilities, and inner completeness, guiding you to use them to reinforce the belief that you are whole and enough just as you are.

You Are Complete

Do you believe something or someone is needed to make you feel fulfilled? Write down your thoughts.

1. _____

2. _____

3. _____

MOOD

☹ 🙁 🙁 🙂 😄

Angry Tired Sad Happy Excited

Think about the things or people you often look to for happiness or fulfillment. Do they bring lasting happiness, or do you feel it fades over time?

_____

_____

_____

Reflect on the strengths and capabilities you possess. What are some qualities or talents you have that bring you joy, fulfillment, or a sense of purpose?

_____

_____

_____

Write a list of affirmations that remind you of your own worth, power, and ability to create happiness.

_____

_____

_____

Rewrite Your Happiness Story Here:

(Day):   (Month):   (Year):

Take a moment to pause and reflect: You are already whole, equipped with everything you need—your strength, your dreams, your unique spark—to shape the life you want. What story do you want to tell about yourself moving forward? What joyful moments, bold choices, or quiet victories will you write into your next chapter? Let your inner voice guide you as you imagine the happiness you deserve, knowing it's yours to create.

Desires Overwhelm the Mind: It's Time To Declutter

Let me explain the difference between intentions and desires. When we want to accomplish something, we need intentions, not only desires. Intentions involve focusing on the process and taking organized steps towards achieving our goals. By setting intentions, we approach tasks with a balanced mindset, knowing that the process itself is important in reaching our desired outcome.

Our brains can become addicted to wanting more and more, and the situation becomes overwhelming. Even if we achieve a desire, we lose the pleasure we expected because our brain has already created new desires in the meantime. It's like a never-ending cycle, with one desire leading to another, and so on. As a result, no matter how much we acquire, we still aren't happy because our brain becomes addicted to desiring something we don't have. It's all about balancing your emotions and thoughts. Pay close attention to your mind. Are you generating more desires that you can not manage? Or are you generating intentions one at a time in an organized manner?

Train your mind and soul. If you find yourself with a cluttered mind full of desires, free your thoughts by returning to meditation. Reconnect with your inner power, recharge yourself, and start again.

OBJECTIVE

This exercise helps you declutter your mind from desires and shift toward setting intentional, mindful goals. By clarifying your desires, focusing on the process, and creating actionable plans, you can achieve your goals with greater balance, less stress, and more fulfillment.

Desires and Intentions planner

(Day):

1- Identify Your Desire:

What is something you truly want to accomplish right now?

2. Clarify Your Intention:
Now, shift your focus from just wanting something to why you want it.

I want it because:

3. Focus on the Process:
How can you focus on the journey or process rather than just the outcome?

4. Set Your Plan:
Reak down your intention into actionable steps

5. Balance and Alignment:
How can you create balance between your desires and intentions? Reflect on how staying mindful of the process can help you reach your desired outcome.

6. Reflect and Celebrate the Process
On how setting intentions has helped you approach your desires in a more balanced and meaningful way.

Desires and Intentions planner

(Day):

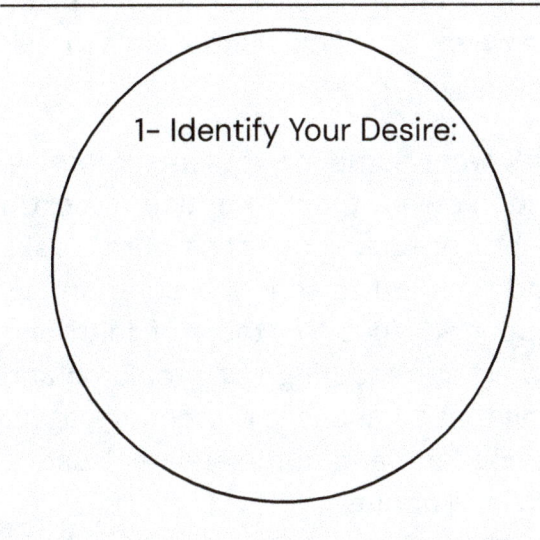

1- Identify Your Desire:

2. Clarify Your Intention:

I want it because:

3. Focus on the Process:

4. Set Your Plan:

5. Balance and Alignment:

6. Reflect and Celebrate the Process

No More Squinting: Trust In A Higher Power

Since I was a little girl, you have always taught me how to pray. We have a prayer for everything. There's a prayer of gratitude when I buy a new dress, a prayer for protection against food poisoning when I'm skeptical about a place or certain food, a prayer for finding parking when it's difficult, and even a prayer for abundance when there's not enough.

I have a prayer for situations where I don't want someone to see something, particularly at the airport counter when I don't want them to notice the extra pound on my luggage scale. I even have a prayer to ensure I don't burn a cake and one to keep my children safe as I send them off to school every morning. "It's not just the prayer itself," Mom responded, "but the tools of faith and intention behind them that matter. It's about surrendering our problems and placing our trust in a higher power, believing that someone is protecting us, our children, and our endeavors. It's about having faith and completely entrusting our concerns to God. That's what true faith is all about."

OBJECTIVE

This exercise helps you bring more faith, intention, and gratitude into your daily life by using simple prayers, letting go of control, and trusting in a higher power.

Prayers Journal

Your Daily Prayers:

Think about your own daily routine and the moments where you feel the need for faith or trust in something greater. Are there situations in your life where you could use a prayer?

Surrendering Control:

How can you let go of worry and trust that things will work out as they should? Write down one area where you can practice this surrender today.

Your Daily Prayers:

The Power of Intention:

What is the intention behind your prayers? Is it for peace, protection, abundance, or something else? Identify the intentions behind the prayers

Creating Empowering Spaces: Reprogramming Beliefs

Let's talk about space. Each person has a space between themselves and the outside world and events. It's within your control to create that space and to decide how you respond to those factors.

Let me tell you a story. There were twin brothers. One was in prison, the other a successful businessman. Both were interviewed and asked the same question: 'How did you end up here?'

The imprisoned brother replied, 'My mother was a drug addict, and my father was an alcoholic. I felt like I had no choice but to grow up lost, following the same cycle of drugs, alcoholism, and bad examples.'

The successful twin responded, 'I had an alcoholic father and a drug addicted mother, but I made a conscious decision not to repeat their mistakes. I wanted to build a family of my own and break free from that destructive cycle.'

These two brothers created different spaces or belief systems for themselves. One belief lifted a person up, leading to their success, while the other brought them down.

OBJECTIVE

This exercise helps you create space between yourself and your circumstances, so you can respond with intention instead of reacting automatically. By practicing mindful awareness, you'll feel more empowered, grounded, and in control of your emotional responses.

Creating Empowering Spaces

The Space Between You and Your Circumstances:

Consider how much space you create between yourself and the external circumstances that impact you.

In what situations do you feel emotionally triggered or reactive?

Empower Your Responses

Reflect on a situation in which How can you change the way you view or respond to that situation? With the new space you have just created, What steps can you take to feel more empowered and in control of your reaction?

Create Positive Space

Think about one small situation from the list above ; where you can consciously create space between yourself and external influences

Creating Empowering Spaces

The Space Between You and Your Circumstances:

In what situations do you feel emotionally triggered or reactive?

Empower Your Responses

Create Positive Space

Cleaning Out Worries: Clear Your Mind

In a cluttered room, there are things you might need, things you no longer need, and trash. The more worrying thoughts you have, the more your mind generates clutter. The more you worry, the more you get trapped in that cluttered room, making it harder to get out.

Once you realize that you're standing in a cluttered room, you start thinking about clearing out some of the mess, and the easier it becomes to get out

OBJECTIVE

This exercise helps you identify the worries cluttering your mind and clear them away using the power of gratitude and intentional imagination, creating space for peace, clarity, and positivity.

Declutter Your Mind

1. Identify the Clutter:

Think about the worries or negative thoughts that are cluttering your mind. What are the things that make you feel overwhelmed or trapped? Write them down.

2. Shift Your Belief About Life:

Reflect on the idea that life is easy and think about the conveniences we have today (e.g., appliances, technology or whatever that you are thankful for making your life easier? Write down one thing in your life that makes things easier or more comfortable compared to the past.

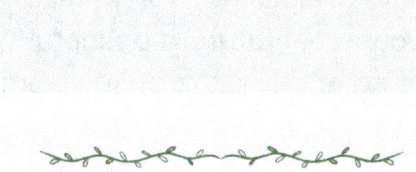

3. Try Meditation:

Take 5 minutes to sit quietly, close your eyes, and focus on your breath. Let go of any worries or thoughts. Simply observe them without judgment, then gently bring your focus back to your breath.

Declutter
Your Mind

4. Acknowledge Worry:

The next time you feel worried, pause for a moment. Acknowledge the worry and say to yourself: "I know what you are. You are worry, and I no longer need you." Then, release the worry and let it go.

5. Replace Worry with Imagination:

After releasing worry, take a few moments to imagine a beautiful scene your ideal future, a peaceful space, or a joyful moment. Picture it vividly in your mind and feel the positive emotions that come with it.

Intentions and Beliefs: The Power to Shape Our Lives

"I want to discuss the belief that you are the architect of your life, with the ability to control what happens externally," Mom said. "Take a moment to reflect on your life, and you'll realize that everything you have is something you once dreamed of, wished for, planned, and ultimately achieved."

OBJECTIVE

This exercise helps you recognize your role and power as the architect of your life by identifying the beliefs and actions that shaped your achievements, and by setting clear intentions to build the future you desire.

Your Role as the Architect of Your Life

DATE: _____

What are 3 things you've achieved in life that you're proud of?
(e.g., personal accomplishments, relationships, career milestones)

How did your beliefs or mindset help you achieve those things?
Were there any limiting beliefs you had to overcome?

How did you respond to challenges or opportunities?
Where did you take control of the situation?

Your Role as the Architect of Your Life

DATE: _____

What are the top 3 goals you want to achieve next?

What specific actions will you take to achieve these goals?

What affirmation can you create to remind yourself that you are the creator of your life?

There's a Gain in every Loss: Focus on the Gains

Let's talk about the gains and losses in life. We tend to focus more on what we lose, but every loss carries a gain. If we shift our focus to the gains, we can find more meaning and joy in our experiences. Dwelling on losses prevents us from fully embracing the blessings, peace, love, and gratitude that come with them.

OBJECTIVE

The purpose of this exercise is to help you shift your perspective by discovering the gain within every loss. By reflecting on past experiences, you can learn to focus on the growth, lessons, and opportunities that came from challenging moments—turning pain into purpose.

Finding the Gain in Loss

Think about significant moments in your life where you experienced a loss. This could be a loss of a job, a relationship, a possession, or any change that felt difficult at the time. What have you lost?

Now, for each loss, write down the gain that came from it, then Focus on the Gains:

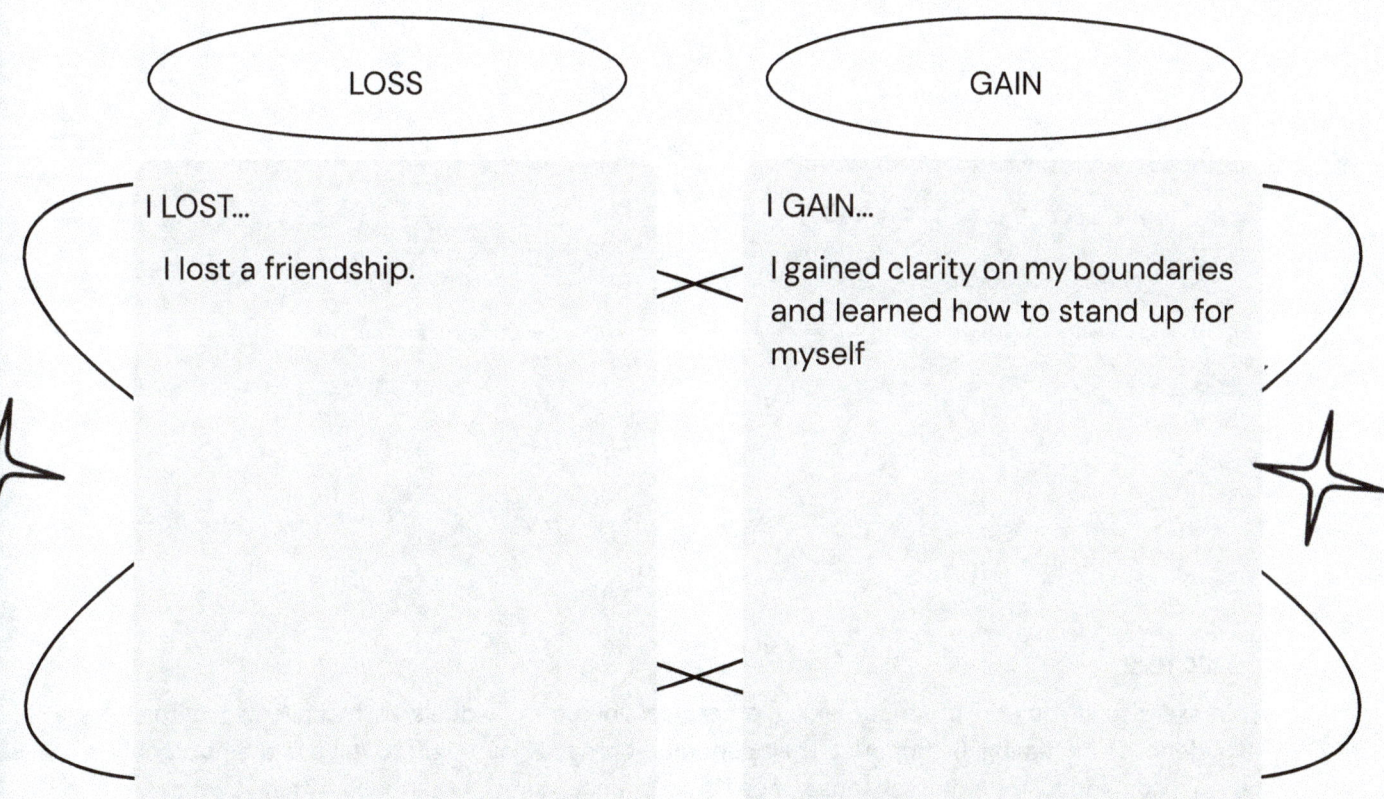

LOSS

I LOST...

I lost a friendship.

GAIN

I GAIN...

I gained clarity on my boundaries and learned how to stand up for myself

Pecan Pie Conversations: The Planets of People

By treating others as separate planets, you remove judgment, criticism, and assumptions about who they are or what they are going through," she said. "You acknowledge that they are entirely distinct from you. In this separation, you no longer compare yourself to others, as you realize that each person's planet is a realm you know nothing about. Instead, you offer respect for their space, decisions, and way of life. You recognize that you have no clue what lies within their planet's depths. Even the closest individuals to you, like your children and your spouse, possess their own separate planets."

OBJECTIVE

This exercise helps you practice seeing others as unique individuals with their own paths, experiences, and timing. By honoring their separate journeys, you begin to release the habit of comparison and foster a deeper sense of self-acceptance, clarity, and peace within yourself.

Viewing Others as Separate Planets

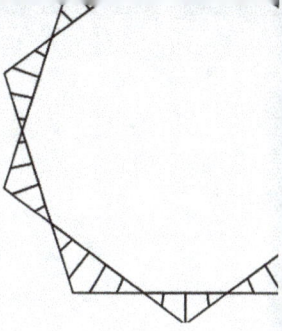

Who in your life have you been comparing yourself to or judging recently?

can you view this person as their own separate planet with a unique life story?

How can you show respect for their individual journey, without assumptions or judgments?

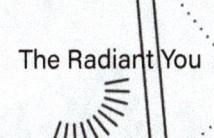

Harmony in Relationships: The Okra Stew of Love

The secret lies in being in harmony with yourself. No matter who your partner is, you will see what you want to see. You are the universe of your own being, and your harmony will reflect what you desire to see. When you are in harmony with yourself, the world will be in harmony with you.

OBJECTIVE

This exercise helps you recognize the power of your mindset and how it affects your relationships. By focusing on your own harmony, you can influence the dynamic without needing to change the other person.

Your Relationship Mindset

Do you or your partner tend to default to complaints, or do you both focus on gratitude and love?

_____   _____

_____   _____

⁂

How Do These Mindsets Affect You?

_____   _____

_____   _____

_____   _____

⁂

How can you adjust your own mindset to create more harmony in the relationship?

_____

_____

_____

Maintaining Strong Beliefs: Align with Actions

Sometimes our beliefs hold us back from doing great things. But when our beliefs align with our actions, we gain strength and harmony. Operating in line with our beliefs empowers us, bringing us closer to ourselves, others, and the universe.

OBJECTIVE

This exercise is designed to help you empower yourself by identifying the core beliefs that guide your life—and evaluating whether your daily actions reflect those beliefs. When your actions align with your values, you feel more grounded, confident, and in control of your journey.

Aligning your Beliefs with your Actions

What is a belief you hold that has influenced
your actions, either positively or negatively?

How has this belief shaped your behavior or choices?

How can you change
your actions to align with a more empowering belief?

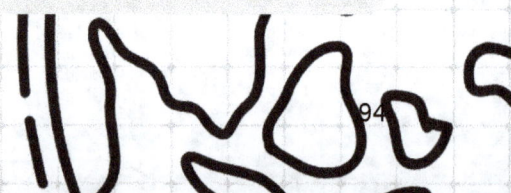

Aligning your Beliefs with your Actions

How do you feel when
your actions align with a belief that empowers you?

Now its your choice, you can either keep
the positive belief, or create a new belief if
it is negative and you want to transform it
to positive one.

We Impact Our Relationships

"You see," she said, her voice filled with faith, "the thoughts we have and the way we talk to ourselves have a profound impact on our relationships. They become a mirror, reflecting back how we perceive ourselves. The way we love ourselves, treat ourselves, and engage in positive self-talk sets the tone for how others treat us."

OBJECTIVE

This exercise helps you explore how you want to be treated in your relationships and encourages powerful shifts in how you treat yourself. By recognizing your needs and nurturing them from within, you begin to create healthier dynamics both internally and with others.

Setting the Tone of Your Relationships

1 How do you want to feel

Reflect on How You Want to feel in your relationships. Take a moment and reflect on your current relationships—whether with family, friends, or a romantic partner. Think about how you want to be treated. (e.g., Loved, Respected, Appreciated, Understood , Cared for, Empowered, Cherished, Accepted, Comforted, Trustworthy, Inspired, Encouraged, Nurtured, Connected, Confident.

I want to feel:

I want to feel:

I want to feel:

I want to feel:

I want to feel:

I want to feel:

I want to feel:

I want to feel:

Setting the Tone of Your Relationships

2   How do you treat yourself

Now, reflect on how you treat yourself.

Do you give yourself the same love, respect, and kindness you wish for from others?

Write down any patterns of self-talk or behavior that may contradict your desires (e.g., negative self-criticism, neglecting your own needs, etc.)

I treat myself with :

I am kind to myself when:

I can improve by:

Setting the Tone of Your Relationships

 3   **Make a commitment to yourself**

Write a commitment statement to yourself, vowing to treat yourself the way you want to be treated. Be specific and realistic in your promises, whether it's taking time for self-care, practicing gratitude, or silencing your inner critic.

I commit to treating myself with love and respect.

I will every day to show myself kindness.

I will to quiet the negative self-talk and focus on being gentle with myself.

Setting the Tone of Your Relationships

4 **What is your action plan**

Identify one specific action you can take today to show yourself love and respect, no matter how small. It could be taking a moment to appreciate yourself, practicing positive self-talk, or setting healthy boundaries.

Example Action:

"Today, I will take a walk, and take time to care for my skin, to show myself love and respect

Setting the Tone of Your Relationships

5 Reflect on the progress

At the end of the week, take time to reflect on your progress. Have you noticed any shifts in how you treat yourself or how you feel in your relationships?

Write down your reflections and continue building on your commitment.

Transforming Worries Into Peace: Take Time to Pray

The worries that creep into your mind result from the negative conversations you're having with yourself. Prayers, on the other hand, are conversations you have with God or a higher power. The former brings you down and doesn't lead you anywhere, while the latter has the potential to transform your circumstances and take you places.

Fear and worry are like gifts from the brain, urging us to pay attention, express gratitude, and redirect our focus. She advised me to thank these feelings for surfacing, forgive them for their attack on my peace of mind, and let them go.

OBJECTIVE

This exercise helps you release fear and worry by redirecting your focus and turning anxious thoughts into calming prayers. It supports a shift in mindset, allowing you to return to a place of peace, presence, and clarity.

Replacing Worries with Prayers

Identify the worries

Write down the worries or negative thoughts you are currently experiencing

- _____

- _____

- _____

- _____

- _____

Replace the worry with a prayer

Write down the worries or negative thoughts you are currently experiencing

Worry: "I'm worried I won't be able to finish this project on time."

Prayer: "Dear higher power, Source, God, I let go of fear and seek your guidance. Inspire me to find ways to finish this project on time

Worry:

Prayer:

Worry:

Prayer:

Worry:

Prayer:

Focus on the prayer instead of the worry
• Whenever the worry resurfaces, pause and repeat the prayer you created. You can also add a feeling of gratitude for the support you're receiving.

Replacing Worries with Prayers

At the end of the week, reflect on how the practice of replacing worry with prayer has shifted your perspective. Write down any changes you've noticed in your thoughts, feelings, and overall mood.

○ _____

○ _____

○ _____

○ _____

○ _____

Ask The Question & Receive The Answer

You know, every question you ask the universe will be answered. The answers will reveal themselves to you. There is a universe inside you, where all your questions and their answers reside. Everyone has this power; can you believe it?

OBJECTIVE

This exercise encourages you to ask meaningful questions and remain open to receiving answers in unexpected ways. It strengthens your intuition

Exercise: Ask the universe any question and you will receive the answers, when you receive it write it down in your answer spaces. Ask away!

Question

How can I bring more abundance into my life?

How do I let go of fear and step into my full potential?

An Answer

Question

How can I be more present in my relationships?

An Answer

Question

An Answer

Exercise: Ask the universe any question and you will receive the answers, when you receive it write it down in your answer spaces. Ask away!

Question

An Answer

Question

An Answer

Question

An Answer

Dreams Do Come True: Prepare Yourself

Have you ever had a dream for a very long time, and when it finally came true, you felt thrilled at first, but then you looked around and thought, 'Is that it? Is this how I am supposed to feel?'

When we attract something in life, we also attract the accompanying feelings. Imagine someone feeling down and depressed because they hate their current job. They desperately want to find another job that brings them happiness. Even when that new job becomes a reality, however, their feelings of depression and dissatisfaction tag along. That's why they continue to feel the same, even in a changed situation.

It all comes down to the preparation. Before attracting what you want, start by preparing the emotional ground. Cleanse and declutter any unwanted emotions.

OBJECTIVE

This exercise prepares you for the emotional readiness needed when your dreams come true. It helps you create an internal environment that is open, aligned, and fully prepared to receive the success, joy, and abundance you've been working toward.

Prepare Your Emotional Ground

Identify Your Dreams and Projects:

Write down the dreams and projects you wish to accomplish, big or small:

[Dream/Project 1]

[Dream/Project 2]

[Dream/Project 3]

[Dream/Project 4]

[Dream/Project 5]

Experience the Emotions:

How do you feel upon completing this dream or project?
Do you feel relieved, happy, proud, or at peace?
Is it a calming feeling, a burst of joy, or a moment of pride?
Imagine those emotions flooding your body and mind.

Reflect on Any Residual Feelings:

As you imagine your success, do any lingering negative feelings or doubts arise (e.g., worries, dissatisfaction, fear)?

Are there any emotional "clutters" from past experiences you need to clear before fully embracing your success?

Take a moment to let go of these emotions. Acknowledge them, thank them for their lesson, and release them.

Prepare Your Emotional Ground:

Now, before you begin working toward your goals, ask yourself:

- Are you mentally and emotionally ready for the feelings that success will bring?

- What emotions or states of mind will help you stay aligned with your dreams and ensure that the fulfillment feels as good as you imagine? (e.g., gratitude, patience, excitement, joy).

Create an intention for each dream or project that will keep you grounded

[Dream/Project 1]

Dream/Project 2]

[Dream/Project 3]

[Dream/Project 4]

[Dream/Project 5]

Closing Thought:
Remind yourself that emotional preparation is just as important as physical action. When your emotions are aligned with your desires, you will attract and experience the success more deeply and authentically.

The Reflection of the Mind: Shaping Your Experiences

Try to wipe the spot on your face, not the one on the mirror this time. Everything, and I mean everything, is a reflection of what's in your mind. Gratitude is the secret, It's the only way to slow down your negative thinking and silence the crying baby in your head.

That's why the prayers we say when we first open our eyes in the morning are reminders to be grateful. 'Thank you, God, for giving us another day to wake up and be alive.' Train yourself to say a prayer upon waking and initiate a change from your default thoughts toward gratitude.

OBJECTIVE

This exercise helps you shift your focus inward by recognizing that your outer world is a reflection of your inner thoughts. It encourages you to start each day with gratitude, training your mind to silence negativity and replace default thoughts with appreciation. By doing so, you begin to clear the "mirror" of your life—not by fixing what's outside, but by healing what's within.

Gratitude Practice

Gratitude for a New Day:

....

....

....

Gratitude
for Health:

Gratitude
Family:

Gratitude for Protection and
Guidance:

Gratitude for
Relationships:

Gratitude for Joy:

....

....

....

....

Gratitude for money:

Gratitude for the
Simple Things:

....

....

....

....

Gratitude Weekly Reflection

What inspired me this week?

_____

_____

A moment that made me smile: Something I did well:

What am I looking forward to next week?

_____

_____

10 things I am grateful for this week:

1 _____

2 _____

3 _____

4 _____

5 _____

6 _____

7 _____

8 _____

9 _____

10 _____

Embracing the Gifts Within: Nurturing Negative Emotions

Let's say you wake up feeling angry. That anger and rage flow through your veins, and if you ignore those feelings, they will manifest in events. You'll encounter people who are angry with you—a boss getting upset, witnessing arguments, or even a car accident with people screaming at each other. If you ignore the anger, it will manifest in your body as pain. You might develop a headache, toothache, or back pain. The more you ignore or try to numb the pain with temporary relief like painkillers, the stronger it may become, this time in the form of diseases.

Once you experience negative emotions, whether it's anger, sadness, or worry, and you begin to see the cycle of negative events unfolding, stop right there. Embrace and welcome those negative emotions, receiving them with gratitude for surfacing. Write them down and ask them questions—where they came from, why they are here, and what message they bring. Write down the answers. Ask and write, even if it may seem silly, for the sake of your mental health.

OBJECTIVE

This exercise is designed to help you become more aware of your emotions, understand their messages, and release any negative energy in a healthy way.

Emotion Tracker

1. Identify Your Emotion:

What emotion are you feeling right now?

2. Trace the Source:

Reflect on what might have triggered the emotion you are feeling. Identifying the root cause helps you gain clarity.

3. Welcome the Emotion:

Instead of resisting the emotion, try to welcome it and explore it. Understanding it can reduce its intensity.

4. Feel it:

What does this emotion feel like in your body?

Is there tightness, heat, tension, or any physical sensation associated with this emotion?

5. Ask Questions:

Why do you think this emotion is showing up?

Is it a reaction to something in the present or a reminder from the past?

What message do you think this emotion is trying to communicate to you?

Is there something you're meant to learn or address through this feeling?

Emotion Tracker

6. Releasing or Shifting the Emotion:

Shift the emotion in a healthier direction. Examples:Talking with someone, journaling, physical activity, creative expression.

7. Reflection:

After completing the exercise, reflect on how the process of acknowledging and exploring your emotion affected you.

Emotion Tracker

1. Identify Your Emotion:

2. Trace the Source:

3. Welcome the Emotion:

4. Feel it:

5. Ask Questions:

Emotion Tracker

6. Releasing or Shifting the Emotion:

7. Reflection:

The Matrix of Societies: You Have Options

When you have options and create more of them for yourself, you're aware of possibilities, and you become stronger and happier. If a job, a city, or even a country isn't working for you, there are countless alternatives out there. You have the power to go anywhere in the world. That's the mindset I want you to adopt.

"By doing so, you'll pave the path to freedom. Some people believe they can only do one job or live in one place, but they are unknowingly imposing limitations upon themselves, blindly following a predetermined path due to their inability to see the array of options available."

OBJECTIVE

This exercise will help you become aware of areas in your life where things may not be working and encourage you to explore new possibilities. By identifying alternatives, you can begin to create a path to freedom and fulfillment.

Exploring Your Possibilities Embracing Freedom

Reflect on what isn't working for you right now? Think about the areas where you feel stuck, unhappy, or limited.

Now, let's explore alternatives. Be open-minded—this is about imagining the countless possibilities available to you. There are no limits! Use the space below to write down at least 3 alternatives or options for how you might approach the situation

Choose one option from your list above. What's the first step you can take to move toward that possibility? The goal is to take small, actionable steps to explore these alternatives. What's one action step you can take today to toward a new possibility?

By completing this worksheet, you're reminding yourself that there are always options available to you—whether it's a job, a location, or simply a change of mindset. Embrace the freedom of exploring new opportunities. You can do this!

First step:

Live In The Moment: Remember The Memories

The more experiences you go through, the more you can fully appreciate life. Remember the good memories without dwelling in them. Create new ones by living in the now and appreciating every step of your journey. That's my advice to you.

OBJECTIVE

This exercise is designed to help you reflect on the past with gratitude, create meaningful experiences in the present, and stay mindful of your current journey.

Reflecting on the Past

Instructions:

1- Think of a positive memory that you often find yourself dwelling on. Maybe it's a time when things felt simpler, or you miss the way things were.

What is one memory you
often find yourself reflecting on?

Memory:

How does this memory make you feel?

Feelings:

Reflecting on the Past

2- Creating New Experiences

Now think about how you can create new positive experiences in your life, right now.

What is one thing you can do today
to create a new, meaningful memory?

New experience idea:

Reflecting on the Past

3- Staying Present

Choose a small task you do daily and practice being fully present while doing it.

What's one task you can be mindful of today?

Task:

Reflecting on the Past

4- Embracing the Journey

Think about how you can appreciate your current life and stay open to the journey ahead.

What is one thing you can do to stay grounded in the present moment today?

Action step:

The Weight of Responsibility: We Were Made for Joy

When life becomes overwhelming, and things aren't falling into place, reconnect and take a moment to close your eyes, breathe deeply, and ask for the higher power to flow through you. Soon, you'll witness the manifestation of your desires. Life is not meant to be shouldered alone.

OBJECTIVE

This exercise encourages you to pause and reconnect with yourself and a higher power when life feels overwhelming.

Releasing the Burden

1. What is currently weighing you down.

   It might be a challenge, a worry, or something you feel is not falling into place.

2. Reconnect

   Now, close your eyes, breathe deeply, and ask for the higher power to flow through you.

3. Take a moment of silence here, and then write down any feelings or insights that arise.

   _____

   _____

   _____

Reminder

Revisit This Exercise When Needed I

Whenever you feel overwhelmed, return to this exercise. Taking a moment to pause and reconnect can help you regain peace and perspective.

Embracing Emotional Resilience: Navigating Separation

Instead of shielding our emotions from the pain of separation, explore proactive strategies. Filling my schedule to distract myself from her impending departure wouldn't offer genuine protection—it would merely serve as a temporary escape. Being proactive, on the other hand, involved learning how to uplift oneself during moments of sadness and disconnection.

Identifying activities or practices that uplifted the spirit, such as listening to a favorite song that ignited joy, engaging in a prayer that fostered a positive sense of connection with the soul, watching a meditation video that offered solace, or simply embracing moments of silence that restored inner calm. These proactive measures.

OBJECTIVE

This exercise is designed to help you practice self-compassion and become more aware of your feelings around separation. It encourages you to support yourself during these times, reflect in a healthy way, and proactively navigate separation with care and resilience.

Separation & Self Compassion

Take it All Out
"Feel it to heal it."

What am I feeling right now?

- _____
- _____
- _____
- _____

Let it be messy:

Have I cried, yelled, or written it out?

☐ Yes ☐ Not yet (plan a time)

Where do I feel it in my body?

_____

_____

_____

_____

Separation & Self Compassion

> **The Three Sheets of Separation**
>
> **Permanent Separation (Death, divorce, endings with no return)**

Who or what are you separating from

_____

Name your situation. Honor it. Reflect intentionally

_____

_____

_____

What hurts the most?

_____

_____

What do I wish I could say?

_____

_____

How can I honor and let go? (e.g., ritual, letter, symbolic act)

_____

_____

_____

Separation & Self Compassion

> **The Three Sheets of Separation**
>
> **Temporary physical Distance**
> **(Long–distance relationships, travel,temporary moves)**

What is the situation?

_____

What fears or needs come up during distance?

_____

_____

What helps us stay connected?

_____

_____

Boundaries or routines I can create:

_____

_____

Separation & Self Compassion

The Three Sheets of Separation

Evolving Relationships(Shifts in emotional closeness or priorities)

Examples:

A best friend is having a baby, and you sense the dynamic changing as their focus shifts to parenthood. Your daughter or son is getting married, and your role in their life is shifting from caregiver to supportive observer. A friend is entering a new season— starting a demanding job, or reprioritizing their time. You feel emotional distance growing between you and someone you used to speak with daily.

What relationship is evolving for me right now?

_____

What emotions does this shift bring up (joy, grief,loss,pride, confusion?

_____

_____

_____

What am I resisting or clinging to?

_____

_____

What would it look like to stay open and supportive as the relationship changes?

_____

_____

_____

How can I stay connected while also allowing space?

_____

_____

_____

Separation & Self Compassion

Build Your Uplift Toolbox

What uplifts, nourishes, or calms me when I feel sad or alone?
A song that brings me joy:

_____

A prayer or affirmation:

_____

A meditation or breath work practice:

_____

5–10 minutes of silence or journaling

_____

A walk outdoors or in nature

_____

A creative outlet:

_____

Separation & Self Compassion

Speak It or Share It

Talking brings healing. Plan to speak your truth to:

A trusted friend or family member

A therapist or coach

A voice memo just for me A letter I'll write but not send

Separation & Self Compassion

Weekly Reflection Prompts:

01. What emotion showed up the most this week?

02. What helped me even a little bit?

03. What growth am I noticing in myself?

04. What truth or clarity is becoming visible through this separation

Tip: Revisit this worksheet anytime you're facing a new or recurring separation. Each time you return, your inner strength grows.

Intricacies of Fear: Replacing with Gratitude

Why is it that fear sometimes enters our hearts? I find myself becoming fearful even in the face of small or ordinary things. Worst-case scenarios often creep into my thoughts, weakening me and enveloping me in fear.

"Fear emerges when you are in a low vibration, when you are out of harmony with yourself, when you feel "disconnected," I asked, "then how to reconnect?" "Start with gratitude. Focus"

Start with gratitude," Mom said. "Focus on the things you truly love and are grateful for in your life. It's not about thinking of what you should be grateful for; it's about acknowledging and appreciating the things that genuinely bring you joy.

OBJECTIVE

This exercise helps you acknowledge your fears and consciously replace them with gratitude to shift your mindset and raise your vibration.

Replacing Fear with Gratitude

Identifying Your Fears & Replacing Them with Gratitude

Fear	Gratitude
Fear of failure	I'm grateful for the courage to try.
Getting older/Ageing	Grateful for the clarity that come with each passing year.

Reflecting on the Shift:

Here is a collection of

prayers to guide you—read

them slowly, breathe through

them, and let them bring you peace.

Morning Prayer – Starting the Day

Dear God,
Thank you for this new day. May I walk through it with grace, awareness, and kindness. Help me to stay grounded, centered, and open to your guidance. Let my thoughts be calm, my words be gentle, and my heart be light.

Prayer for When You Feel Overwhelmed

Dear Source of Peace, In this moment of heaviness, I surrender what I can't carry. Calm my mind, ease my breath, and guide my steps. Show me what matters most, and remind me I am held.

Prayer for Letting Go

Divine Presence,
Help me release what no longer serves me— the worry, the fear, the old stories. Let me feel free, light, and open to something new. I trust that letting go creates space for something better.

Prayer for Clarity

God,
Clear my inner noise so I can hear what's real. Speak through my intuition and lead me with your light. Help me make decisions from wisdom, not fear.

Prayer for Love & Relationships

Dear God,
Teach me to love without control and listen without judgment. Help me respect the people in my life as separate souls, each on their own path. May my love be a mirror of your patience and peace.

Evening Prayer – Closing the Day

Thank you for the moments of joy and the lessons in challenge. As the day closes, I release the need to fix or figure out. Let my mind rest and my body be at ease. Wrap me in your peace tonight. Help me rejuvenate every cell of my body with healthy, vibrant energy. Let me wake up refreshed—with clarity, strength, and good news awaiting me.